and some other
third thing.

Elena Faverio, Tessa Permar & Ivy Stevens

to my yertle
love you
e

For Sam and Sarah, and to the fourfooteds
who wrote with us.
TP

For the version of myself I left in 2020
I.S.

Table of Contents

Content Warnings

~Intermission~

Table of Contents cont.

Content Warnings

What's The Whole Deal With This Book?

We three met at the National Theater Institute in 2013. Elena suggested this group at the beginning of Covid as a way to cope/stay engaged/be creative/etc. We generated prompts from conversations, books of writing prompts, writing prompt generator websites, and some from Suleika Jauad's The Isolation Journals. Like a lot of folks, we all started many projects in 2020, but this is one of the few we all actually kept up with. We are intentional about what we're doing: we meet once a week remotely for one hour - unless someone has a conflict and we decide not to meet, or decide to meet for longer. We don't have homework - occasionally we'll "bring in an object" or pick a song to share, but there's no expectation of work being done before the meeting. When we write, we never focus on having any kind of final product - some pieces are left unfinished, and we just move on to write something else if we feel like it. Even this book is not the culmination of all our work; it comes out of wanting to celebrate what we've done so far. This whole vibe is part of why we've been able to stick with it while we fell off of other projects.

We've held these meetings on Thursdays, Sundays, Wednesdays, (but never Saturdays!) because we all work in theater and our schedules vary a lot. We are constantly changing and evolving the format: some days we invite guests, some days we play D&D, sometimes we have a plan, and other times we spend most of our time chatting. In year one, we mostly wrote from prompts and conversations, using what was happening around us and what was going on in our internal worlds. In year two, we did a lot of accountability writing - we all had other things we were working on, and used our weekly hour for that. In year three, we have expanded our structure and sources of inspiration, using more nontraditional sources to help us generate work.

We decided to make a book at this stage, because at the start of year three we looked back and realized we had generated a large amount of work. We thought it would be nice to collect some of it in one place. We had previously discussed starting a blog, which we also have done, but Ivy wanted something she could physically hold as well, and Tessa and Elena said fine. We've been friends for ten years, have been writing for three, and this feels like a commemoration of both those things. Common themes emerge as we write: suburbia, dystopia, the environment, technology breakdown, love. As we write about these things, we reflect these ideas back at each other, which helps us imagine them in new and different ways. In writing this book, we hope to share some of that collaborative process with you. We invite you to read, and also to take inspiration from anything that catches your imagination.

We also wanted to take this moment to call out the friends and co-conspirators who have joined us on this journey, either as writers or prompters or DMs. Cas Koenig, Shanan Wolfe, Nick Osbourne, Abby Birkett, and Ben Stevens.

What is the other third thing?

If you write long enough, you may notice that you start to write about the same things over and over. We'd usually say "we" and speak from our own experience, but we think this is something common to all writers. Things tend to come up. Not always overtly, not always obviously, but suddenly you start to notice themes. Threads you can tangle in your fingers and think, huh. Let me pull this towards me, let me try to trace this back to the beginning.

As the three of us have written together over the past three years, many themes and ideas have cropped up in our writing (see above). One theme that we didn't mention above (and which inspired the title for this volume!) is threes. Threes, in fact! The three of us writing for three years, three is a magic number, trilogies and triptychs and trios and triangles. A perfectly balanced shape, the strongest shape. A shape that stands poised on one single point and threatens to collapse at the slightest provocation. As you read this collection of works, we invite you into yet another lovely and delicate trio: the one that exists in this moment between us, you, and the words you are about to read. Go forth, be weird, enjoy.

~~The Wiyrd Systers~~ ~~Wieiyrd Systers~~ Weird Systers

Are there more wheels or doors in the world?
Let's all say what we think on the count of three, okay?
1 2 3
-

If one person says doors and two say wheels read this:
Like time and civilization, all things roll down hill.
Gravity is inevitable.
Newton knows about this, so does Johnny Appleseed.
Like the universe and a wheel in a dusty vacuum, all things roll
until they reach the bottom.
The ending is inevitable.
Everyone knows this. Even the wind. Even the stars in the sky.

If one person says wheels and two say doors read this:
Aren't you getting damp, out there in the rain?
A newspaper isn't a great substitute for an umbrella.
You should come inside. Come in from the cold.
It's too cold out, so we're opening hotels and Airbnbs and empty
Montauk mansions for the homeless.
When the nights rise again over 40 degrees, we'll turn them out into
the streets again
Let them build up cardboard cities with newspaper blankets
so we can burn them down and wash them away, into the storm
drain.
Take off your shoes.
We're not a "no shoe household" all the time, but your sneakers are
damp.
I'll stuff them with newspaper, so they'll be dry when you leave.

If everyone says wheels:
Congratulations! Good things are coming your way. Can you feel
them, floating in on the spring wind?
The pinwheel is spinning again, and the birds are waking you up at

the ass crack of morning.
Get up, bitches! They carouse into the golden 6 AM.
Get the fuck up! Good news is on the way! It's spring again
And everything is green and gold
And the pinwheel is spinning in the gorgeous, gorgeous breeze.

If everyone says doors:
Maybe this is how it is -
you're always going out of the room.
There you go again, clearing the dishes after the holiday meal
You're in the kitchen now, but a moment ago you were in the
dining room.
Chasing the dog down the hallway into the breezeway into the
driveway -
A door you don't even remember open, left -
Propped by a stone or a brick or a child's shoe.

And you're ducking under stone archways of cathedrals and cave
mouths,
rushing into the tunnel at 80 miles per hour - because it's late and
even the city is sleeping -
Rushing out the other end in the same breath.
Do you feel it?
Even now, you're going out of the room, into the next.
Into the next.

To conclude:
Let's linger for one moment - on the threshold.
On that perfectly balanced point.

Prompt: Are there more wheels or doors in the world?

Meet Me At The Place

It's the place we go when we get off work, but it's not yet time to go home. There's something we don't want to do at home, or someone we don't want to see, and so we have to be somewhere else for a while. It's the place we go to meet up with friends on the weekend, when our houses are too messy for visitors and we don't have time to clean. It's the place you go when your dog has fleas and they need to fumigate so you can't be inside the house for 9 hours this Saturday. It's the place you go for lunch with your coworkers, where you carefully don't talk about your bosses or too much about your home life. It's the place you invite that guy from the coffee shop so you can meet in public and see if you want to ask him on an actual date. Sometimes it's a place you go to be alone, but more often it's a place you go to be in community.

It's a bright place. The lights are low and gentle, perfectly cozy. It has lots of natural light, or it has plenty of lamps. It's open to the sky and has lots of fresh air, but the breeze never ruffles the pages of your book as you read. It's nice and quiet, but you never have to lower your voice when you're there if you're having a good time being loud. It's completely private, you and your date or your friends or your coworkers can always find somewhere to sit that's away from other people. It's not empty, always filled with the reassuring bustling of humanity. It's a public space, you don't have to worry about someone telling you to move on. It's a privately owned space, where you can be sure you won't be interrupted by random passers by. You can simply sit and people watch as the rest of the world moves around you. You can be safe in the knowledge that no one is ever watching you. There's never any trash and it always smells clean. It never feels sterile and you always know your mess is welcome.

There are chairs around tables so you can sit and eat. There are benches facing the walking paths, and benches facing away from everyone. There are lawn chairs like at the pool where you can stretch out and sunbathe. There are easy chairs for you to snuggle up in. There are places to refrigerate your leftovers and charge your phone. There are places to use the bathroom and get a drink of water. There are places to lie down, and they always have clean sheets and pillowcases. You can carry your lunch bowls to the sink and wash them yourself, leaving them in the drying rack where they'll be waiting for you for next time. You can get up from the table when you're done eating and leave everything where it is, the dirty napkins and food scraps and used cups, and it's someone else's job to clean it up. There are fenced in areas where dogs and kids can run around unsupervised with low risk. There are no children or pets allowed, so you don't have to worry about listening to crying or stepping in dog poop. There's a gurgling river, there's a sandy beach with the sound of the ocean, there's fields of wildflowers, there's pristine empty lawn, there's bricked courtyards, there's lush carpet. There's a place to park your bike and you never have to lock it up. You can pull your car right up to the front and there's no motor vehicles allowed.

Everything is accessible to those with mobility issues, there's always informed guides around to help, and no one ever touches your chair without asking. There are areas where you can do sterile injections, there are replacement oxygen carts with wheels, there are hand railings everywhere. There are private rooms where you can breastfeed, and you can feed your baby wherever you like without being stared at. There are places to get a drink and it's a dry campus. There are places to light up and there's absolutely no smoking. There are sharps containers and clean needles for anyone who asks.

It's a place we all know, and all crave. These spaces have been denied us for a long time, but we know them by description. They haven't always been out of reach. There's a collective understanding, a hazy memory we can all just barely make out, we can all swear when we were kids we had a place like this, but for some reason now we can't find it. These spaces don't need to live in our memories. We can breathe them back to life, exhale them into being with that most threatening act, imagination. We want to spend time with one another, want to take care of each other, want to celebrate our shared lives in shared spaces. Want to pray and eat and laugh and read and bike and run and live in community. So close your eyes and imagine the place where you'll meet me.

Prompt: Third Spaces

NEWS TO ME

I've been expecting your call for years now
Both elated and deflated when it doesn't come
I hope that I am growing into a softer and greener self,
That I have less moments of glitching one inch to the right of my
skin like
Why are you this way when you know it's not so deep
And deep
I have collated the mistakes in with the good things
And I am no longer worried about where they stack up
So at night, I sleep whenever I am tired and do not lie awake
There is the future, ahead of me
Like a road
And I don't know where it ends or what happens on the way
But I am not afraid to walk
Can it really be that simple? I ask in the quiet moments when
dread has edged away
And I can just sit in the perfect, temperate, breezy summer
And there are not too many bugs
Can it really be that simple?

Prompt: Write a breaking news story for today

Twenty Twenty:
(connection issues)

- You're on mute. You unmute yourself. You're still on mute. You speak, but you cannot hear yourself.
- Your video keeps turning itself off and back on. Your background looks a little blurry – did you leave motion blur on? You don't think you left motion blur on.
- "Can you hear me? Great, then just to finish what I was saying ah – oh – to continue te – my – ar – "
- Everyone has been sent to breakout rooms, but there doesn't seem to be anyone in yours. When you try to rejoin the main room, your Zoom crashes.
- The others cannot see you. You move to some natural light. They still cannot see you. You turn on the overhead light. No better. You buy a ring light, and they still cannot see you. Your face is shrouded in darkness. The reflection of the ring light glows in your eyes.
- One of the video streams is frozen. The rest of you joke about poor internet, a storm rolling through. Minutes later they're still frozen. You move on without them, wait for them to rejoin. Their feed never drops. They're frozen. Did they just move? Have they ever not been frozen? You start to feel chilly.
- "Aw, is that your dog in the background? He's such a big boy!" You don't have a dog.
- You have been in this room for hours. You have been in this room for days. You are hungry. You finished your tea days ago. There is no water. The heat is going.
- You can hear a siren in the background of someone else's video. Or is that outside your house? The siren gets louder. It's coming from all directions at once. Your mind is filled by siren sound.
- Occasionally your friend's video seems to jump, and you mention it to him. "Its just a glitch", he mutters through a clenched jaw. "Its

just a glitch." He glitches again. His eyes grow haunted. "Its just a glitch."

- Singing happy birthday

Prompt: 3 Prompts - Modern Day Curses

2:53 AM

During the night, I sneak over to the acro yoga studio.
I do this at exactly 2:53 AM, because it's a seven minute walk to the studio,
if I'm moving at a speed that isn't suspicious.
And most murders take place around 3:00 AM.
They say this is because the human body is at its lowest natural biorhythm.
All floppy and invertebrate.
Vulnerable. That's the word I was looking for.
I don't know what I said invertebrate.
It takes a lot of spine to sneak towards the acro yoga studio at 2:54 AM.
By the way, is it possible to move at an unsuspicious speed down a dimly lit suburban street at 2:54 AM?
Excuse me, 2:55 AM now.
One time, my neighbor Pam (that bitch) called the cops on me for standing at my mailbox.
I decided to open a letter that was marked "IMPORTANT"
and it was, actually, important
so I stood there reading for about 10 minutes, during which time Pam (that absolute bitch)
who has seen me everyday for the last 28 years,
decided there was some crazed criminal stealing my mail.
Those are Pam's words, not mine. I read them in the police report.
"Crazed criminal."
Would a crazed criminal be moving stealthily through the suburban night at 2:58 AM towards the sleeping, floppy, tender, invertebrate, defenseless acro yoga studio?
Maybe.
All I know is this: it's it or me, tonight. This ends now.
I could almost do it, once.
The linoleum and the seersucker,

The fucking in missionary position,
The casualness of backyard beekeeping, killing hives year after year without thought,
The lawns, trimmed to "¼ inch, all by the same ride on mower
The rounded hedges,
Coffee o'clock, and it's five o'clock somewhere, and
"God Bless this Home" on new wood made to look like old wood. Almost.
It's 2:59 AM, and I am standing in front of the acro yoga studio.

Prompt: Greenland (see Prompt list in endnotes)

Hotel Armand

"What is this?"

"This is your room."

"This is not our room."

You're 100%, dead certain that when you made this reservation, you asked for a suite, with a kitchen, a bathroom, and TWO small bedrooms. The room in front of you, at which the friendly front desk gentleman is gesturing, is smaller than your first apartment. There's a desk, a wardrobe, a door that clearly leads to a small bathroom, and one, single queen sized bed. "I specifically reserved a suite for the weekend."

He looks confused, and slightly alarmed. "I'm sorry, you must be mistaken. We don't even have any suites here."

You close your eyes. Okay, so you weren't the one to make the reservation, per se. That was your assistant Danny. But you did have a conversation with Danny, in writing, over email, about your expectations for your accommodations. This weekend is your only break between several long work trips. The last two weeks straight have been nothing but red eye flights and shareholder meetings at random company headquarters in cities all over the country, and the next two weeks will be more of the same. This weekend was your one and only chance to unwind, stop working, and relax for one goddamn second.

You open your eyes and shoot Danny a look.

He catches your eye and splutters, quickly swinging his backpack to the floor and rifling through it. Danny is young, new to the company, having just been assigned to you a few months before this godforsaken series of trips. It had taken some time to get used to one another, as is always the case with new assistants, but things had been working out more or less smoothly on the trip until now. You try your best not to compare him to your old assistant Patricia, who had been superb and had moved on to bigger and better things.

"I'm positive I have the confirmation right here." Danny's carefully not looking at you now, and you're trying very hard to stifle the long-suffering sigh that is working its way through your chest. Finally, he pulls out some slightly crumpled printouts. "Ah! Yes, here. It says 'suite, two rooms, kitchenette...'"

The baggage boy takes the papers, a practiced smile on his face. He looks them over quickly and then turns them around, pointing to the hotel name at the top of the sheet. "This says Hotel Armand. This is the Hotel Almond."

There is a moment of complete silence as you stare at the paper, unblinking, before slowly turning your gaze on Danny. He makes that sputtering noise again, grabbing the papers out of the bellhop's hands. He pulls out his phone, presumably to check the email confirmation against the one in his hands. "I don't understand, is this not 148 North Augusta?"

"This is 148 South Augusta." The man's smile implies that this is a question he has answered more than once in the past. Your chest hurts with the pressure of holding in that sigh. You put a hand to your head and begin massaging your temple.

"Danny. Let's make some calls, alright? Excuse us for a moment." You turn on your heel and stride back down the hall to the front desk area, where you can at least sit while you figure out whether or not to strangle Danny. You'd driven through the evening to get here, thinking longingly of your private suite and cushy bed, and now it is 2am and all you want is some sleep. Danny follows at your heels like a sad puppy, still scrolling through his email.

"I'm so sorry Alex, I don't know how this happened. I checked the address like five times, maybe the GPS auto filled the address without me noticing, you kinda get used to just following those directions without really thinking about it–"

You cut him off. "Just, call the hotel, the real hotel, and let them know we'll be late for our reservation." He nods and scurries out the front doors, taking the call outside. The front desk man returns to his post as you flop down in a recliner.

"If it helps," he says from behind his desk, "that room is available. Last minute cancellation. You're lucky. The music festival is happening this weekend, and most of the hotels around here have been booked up for months."

You put on your most gracious smile and try to keep the annoyance out of your voice. "Thank you, but I really don't think my assistant and I will be taking you up on your kind offer."

"Ah," says the man, raising his eyebrows. "I pegged you for a couple. No pun intended." He laughs a little awkwardly.

You're barely paying attention, having taken out your own phone to check on the rest of your itinerary. "I've no idea what you're talking about." You look up. "A couple? I could be his... well, maybe not his father, but still..." You turn your attention back to your phone, pulling up your GPS to check how far away Hotel Armand is from your current location: 45 minutes, somehow.

"My apologies, it was just a...vibe."

You finally lose the battle you'd been having with the sigh, dropping your face into your hands, as you realize the desk clerk was right: every hotel within a reasonable distance from you is booked solid.

The sliding doors whoosh softly as Danny reenters. You look at his expression and can tell immediately you're not going to like what he's about to say. He knows it too, judging by his posture as he approaches you. "Please tell me the good news."

He opens his mouth, then pauses, seeing something in your face. You try to
smooth your expression. You've often been told that you get a little scary looking when you're mad - something in the eyes. It's not an intentional thing, and you've been working on it. Not enough, apparently. When you're tired you have a somewhat looser grip on your emotions.

After a moment he continues, in an apologetic tone. "The Hotel Armand has a very strict check in policy, and as it is now after

2am–" You wince. "–the suite has been considered forfeit and offered to another guest."

You can feel a nerve on your forehead twitching, and you rub your eyes from a mixture of frustration and exhaustion. Danny perches on the chair beside yours, continuing with a nervous energy. "I called several other hotels in the area, but none of them have any rooms available, let alone a suite."

"I know Danny." You lean back in the armchair, giving up on your phone and letting your hand fall into your lap. "I was just checking availability as well. There's nothing."

Danny sits back in his chair, looking slightly relieved. "Armand is only 45 minutes away, let's just…show up, and demand they give us a room! I'll fix this Alex, I swear I'll figure it out."

You glance at the man behind the desk, who seems to be carefully not listening to everything you're saying. "You're positive that's the only room you have available?" He looks up immediately, and raises a keycard. You knew he was eavesdropping. You sigh, from the bottom of your soul, and heave yourself out of the armchair. At the desk you snatch the keycard out of his hand, pat your pockets until you locate your wallet, and put the company card on the counter. Danny rises from his chair to follow you, looking resigned. The clerk runs your card and hands it back. "Do you at least have another bed we could bring in? A cot? A sleeping bag?" You're only half joking.

"I'm very sorry, sir," says the clerk, looking rueful. "All our resources have gone to the out of towners coming in for this music festival. If I could get you something else I would. But unfortunately it's true - there's only one bed."

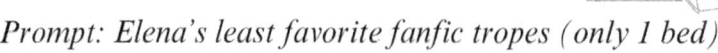

Prompt: Elena's least favorite fanfic tropes (only 1 bed)

The Sleeping Cult

Before she even opens her eyes Lee can feel the intensity of white sunlight pounding at the doors of her eyelids. Her hands grip the blankets on top of her, and she pulls the heavy fabric up around her chin like a lion's mane. She sets her jaw into the layers of cloth and lets out a sigh through her nose. Open your eyes, she tells herself. Just a crack. This she manages, and sees through a web of lashes, that the space around her is just as bright as it feels. Lee closes her eyes again, flinching a little. Her body curls around itself as she rolls to one side, bargaining with the universe for 15 more minutes.

As if the universe decided to answer, her room is suddenly dim. The pressure and the soft pain under her eyelids are instantly lifted. Her limbs ease to welcome sleep back in. And then she hears footsteps.

Her eyes peel open and she's up on her elbows, squinting toward the sound. A shape darker than the others, no it's two shapes, two figures stand against the wall, their eyes locked on hers.

Dammit Sarah, this isn't how it's supposed to go, one figure says to the other.

Then to Lee she explains, This isn't how it's supposed to go. We mis-estimated your waking time. Sarah is still training. I apologize. It looks like you aren't due to wake for another hour and 58 minutes. Forgive us, we'll be going.

Lee watches them turn toward a doorway hung with more thick fabric. As they reach the doorway, it occurs to Lee that she may be awake. This might not be a dream.

Wait, please! She calls, and the figures turn.

Where? Where are we?

The figures glance at each other, their expressions arguing without words. The elder figure turns in decision.

Return to your sleep Lee, we will meet you when you wake.

It's said like a command, but also like a prophecy. Lee relaxes back into the pillows and lets her eyelids wilt toward closing. Now she is sure that she is dreaming. How else would that stranger know her name.

Prompt: Cult

The Taste of Chocolate

How do you describe the feeling of eating chocolate? And not like Hershey's or dollar store chocolate, but proper creamy cocoa chocolate that coats your mouth. Can you describe a taste? Chocolate melting in your mouth feels like the softest, comfiest blanket being laid across your tongue. It smells like rich damp earth, a temperate forest in springtime, mixed with just a hint of cool metal, like the cover of a laptop that hasn't been turned on in a while or those smooth metal railings in your middle school. Biting into a piece of chocolate feels like a light crack, like popping a joint in your knuckle, or the feeling of holding a green, growing thing in two hands and pulling it apart. Not sharp, more like a tug and release. Chewing chocolate feels like – you should not do it, you should let it melt in your mouth, but if you're going to chew it. It feels like a gentle giving way, enough resistance to feel like you're trying, but not enough to make it feel like work. Chocolate makes you want to chew it, to eat it the way you eat other things, but if you do that then it's gone too soon and you don't get to savor it. So eating chocolate is like feeling the impulse to proceed as normal and receive quick gratification, but convincing yourself to prolong the experience in order to enjoy it more intimately. Letting chocolate melt in your mouth is like making a decision to commit yourself to one experience for an extended time, to choose to savor a simple pleasure. Eating a piece of chocolate is like going into a warm, dark room, laying down in the softest blankets, smelling earth and metal, and deciding to stay there a while.

Prompt: Touching luxury

1. BTS
2. Police reform on LI since EO203
3. Being a sister
4. Tamora Pierce Books
5. My cat, Yertle
6. The 7 times table
7. Disney Princess Movies
8. Fanfiction searches
9. Questioning identities
10. ATLA

MY CAT YERTLE

In my softest and most precious times
I can understand how lucky I am
to sit warmly in bed, with a perfect cat clawing her way across my stomach
Nails clipping awkwardly into the duvet
Knees angled and awkward like a chicken
Strutting and yowling at 2 AM
It is no one's fault but my own
That she believes 2 AM is the perfect time to complain
Or announce her undying love in caterwauling tones
As I was the fool who woke, one night, from woolen dreams
To pull her close and tell her she was perfect
And pet her velvet ears and let her know that I will wake up when she calls me
In my softest and most painful times
I can understand how brief and stacked the time is
We have had wonderful days of kittenhood and claws out
Of blown-eyed catnip wondering and nighttime mouse haunt stalking
And years of coming home with a backpack or a suitcase or nothing

To know that she remembers me still and will still crawl warm into
my lap
And let me pet her little belly
I don't want to lose this, I think up into the midnight
As she curls awkwardly on the floor in a pile of my clothes
Or sprawled across a cardboard box that I bought with things in it
for me
I don't want to lose this little life
Why did you come into my life this way?
And make yourself so perfect
And so fragile
And so wild
That even a wind could blow you far from me
And nothing but death could come between us two
My cat doesn't care.
Even now
She sits on the floor and licks her asshole
And understand that it's enough.
All of it, taken as one.
This soft and precious time
It is enough.

Prompt: 10 things I know about & 10 things I know nothing about

The Shmouse

Shmouse: The shmouse is like an oldworld mouse only it is immediately distinguishable by its larger rounder ears, mimicking oldworld satellite dishes. The ears have the ability to pan wide open like a plate, or telescope into narrow listening tubes, like two half open umbrellas. Their nostrils are also larger, giving them the expression of a cow who has just inhaled a fly. Whiskers are the same as always. Coloring: now this is where the shmice have diversified. Instead of a smokey gray range like the oldworld door mouse, shmice have developed coloring that mimics the specific surfaces of wood and trees. There are different shmice for different trees. Some display the inky greens of wet lichen and prefer old oaks and maples. Some have even developed grain-like texture to their fur and live in barns, shacks, and anywhere with exposed planks. But the most common shmice in our region prefer the birch. Their coats resemble the color of snow with specs of damp soil. If you look closely even their noses are the color of watered down milk and their eyes, only dark flecks on their white bodies. The tails, although shorter, are white as well, making them keen to fully surprise you on your first culling of bark.

Prompt: The Quiet Year, PostGame (see prompt list in endnotes)

Wild and the Opposite of Wild

Have you ever heard a pack of coyotes in the middle of the night? Our house backs onto a bit of forest, honestly I'm not sure how far back the uncultivated land goes. Eventually it must run into the city, but I suppose it could be a few miles before then. Anyway, at the edge of our manicured lawn, just where it meets the forest, the bushes and trees make a little archway, just tall enough for a person to pass under if crouched. On the other side of this little passageway is a small clearing, in the middle of that clearing a large pine tree.

I have this desire to manicure this area, to make the archway more intentional. Sweep the bramble from the clearing, put out some stumps or a picnic table under the pine tree. I'd take my tea out there on cool mornings and listen to the birds sing. I'd leave the crusts of my toast for crows to eat, and they'd become my friends and leave me little presents. When I drop my wedding ring in the cushion of fallen pine needles, they'd see the glint off the sapphires and pick it up, leaving it on the table for me to find tomorrow morning.

On the other hand, one of the things that makes the clearing so enchanting is that it happened naturally. No one planted those bushes, no one pruned them away to make a yonic opening into the underbrush. There's something magical about looking at this little portal and thinking 'this looks like a magic place'. Clearing it out and putting up some seating would mess with its natural beauty. Plus, the moment I actually pass through the portal and I'm faced with the roots that trip me up and the sticky tree sap that falls from the pine and just so much deer shit everywhere, some of the magic might be lost.

But that's not what really keeps me away. Every couple of nights we hear a pack of coyotes. We live on a pretty populated street, near a city, but that doesn't seem to deter them. I've yet to see one with my own eyes, but hearing them is almost worse. Their high pitched, almost whining howls will start from the east side of the house, then get echoed on the west, finally coming from deep in the forest along past my magic portal. Though I've never seen anything more frightening than a bunny in our yard, standing out there in twilight as the sun dips below the horizon and the temperature creeps down, being surrounded on three sides by the shrieking of wild beasts....it makes me appreciate my nice manicured lawn. I try not to run as I turn my back on the bramble arch and move toward the warm light spilling from my kitchen door.

Prompt: Something about animals

How to Be an Islander

Salt, sand, moss, dewdrop webs, that collective cicada engine sound, thick tall sick-looking trees, crinkled fragile eyes, cutting themselves from tears with belittling jokes. Family men, the round bulge of their jaws jutting toward the next thing they have to do. A lot of witches. Young witches spinning indigo yarn, bearded ladies with new Spring lambs, glittering rich crones, all of them in linen blouses shaped like bat wings.

Kids with fruit punch rings around toothy wet mouths, screeching at the edge of hilarity and terror. The deer, always moving around us like a current. Squawks from live flocks and the ghosts of old birds. Mulch-caked boots. Sand-caked boots. Blood-caked boots. Snow and pine-needle and splinter-caked boots.

And now and then, more than there used to be, suits. An occasional tie. Wampum jewelry on white skin leathered by the sun, sterling silver charms jangling on cream-colored freckled wrists. New dogs on leashes walking down my road. Different kinds of phone calls to the office now. We don't need jobs, we need places to live.

And a new generation. Audra Lorde quoted on the school board. Skinny kid on the sidewalk looking like a Brooklyn-born. My coworker used to do marketing for Asos. Her husband is in film. Power Lesbians? Amy Schumer running vigils for Black Lives Matter on Sundays over zoom?

I just figured it out. If it were here, if it were real, if she were us and we were them, it would, simply, all be happening outside. Everything here that is us, is outside. That is why I don't belong here either. Maybe I can pronounce Chappaquiddick and Pohogonot but my life is lived indoors. It's not so much about birthplace or skin-tone or occupation. Once you become an outdoor person, that is when you become an islander.

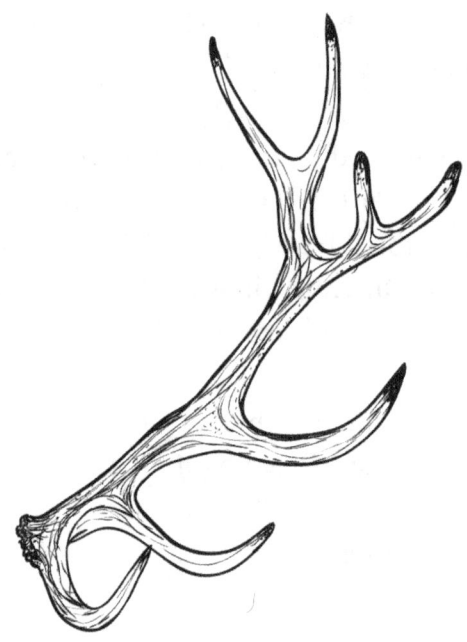

Prompt: Looking at your homestead from a distance

PLASTIC/BATSU

Everyone needs to leave because another show starts in 30 minutes
The audience trundles begrudgingly out the side exit no one knew
existed until this moment
I'm sitting at a tall table, letting my legs kick over the sticky venue
floor
My buddy is in the show and I came to see him
He lost the game where you need to rhyme while rapping
And stuck his fingers into 10 mousetraps
"That sounds like the worst one," I told him, when I heard about
what his job was like
"It's a specific kind of pain," he said.
I know a thing or two about that.
Before the show, I got talking to the wizened old lady sitting across
from me
She was auditioning to be part of it and they told her to stick
around for the show
"To see what I'd be getting into," she cackled.
Really, not all old women are like witches, but this one was.
Some young women are like witches too.
An old memory: one of my first classes in drama school surfaces,
blood beading a sharp cut you've just realized connected with flesh
Our teacher, a witch of a different breed, calls us one by one into a
circle and gives us characters
The girls go, tiny, pale waifs of the UK who have never seen the sun
Wide eye and knobby-kneed and always blushing with
embarrassment down their necks
Girls from California, all boobs and fake teeth
Girls from New York, reedy and ready to stomp your face in with
platform shoes
Our teacher calls out to them, "Artemis, goddess of the hunt"
"Tinkerbell"
"Aphrodite"

"Helen of Troy"
"Titania, Queen of the Fairies"
When I enter the circle, she looks at me and calls
"The Wicked Witch of the West"
I make them laugh by giving my best Almira Gultch cackle and
after we finish,
the teacher says:
Isn't it interesting how some stereotypes come easily to some
people?
There's a specific kind of pain, like looking down at the Nike
swoosh scar on the first knuckle of my right hand and knowing that
it's been there longer than memory
The sort that looks almost like the color of flesh, just slightly
yellow, just slightly hot to touch
The one where I turn my head by accident and catch my profile in
the shop window
The outline of my chin in the background of someone else's
Facebook photo
That thought that circles overhead like a twister
I land on my feet on the sticky venue floor of BATSU
And you can't crush the witch when you are the witch.
Most of the audience has completed their begrudging shuffle out
into the New York night and a short bald man is frantically
collecting plastic cups off tables and dumping them in the trash
I catch his eye and he smiles sheepishly
"It seems like such a waste of plastic, but I really don't know what
else to do. They won't recycle them if they haven't been rinsed and I
just don't have time"
I can make small talk when I want to, so I say
"I don't know who would be responsible for it but you could look
into biodegradable plastic alternatives"
The man stops and really looks at me
"I'm the owner. I've never thought of it. What a good idea."
I go back to BATSU a full year later to see my buddy

And he loses the game where you need to rhyme while rapping
And sticks his fingers into 10 mousetraps
This time, he comes up with a mouse trap snapped to each finger
He only got six last time
"I was so close," he said to me after the show.
"I almost had them all."
I drink water out of my plastic cup and scream and scream and
scream.

Prompt: Literally no one can remember which prompt it was lol

Dreams and Fantasies

I have this fantasy of being squished. Typically this fantasy takes one of two forms. The first looks like a cartoon. There is a machine with a giant roller on the front that presses wet pavement. I desire to lie on something soft and be pressed, rolled, squeezed flat like dough. I want to pass the gluten windowpane test. My energetic toothpaste tube that contains all of my ickiness would be squeezed until flat, and I would be dry, empty, and clean.

The other fantasy is similar but not the same. I wish to hibernate underground - safely. I wish to become one with the dirt, to complete a life cycle under the ground. To be buried where I am today, at the peak of my life, left to ripen, mold, and disintegrate into fungus food. Then to seed, take root, sprout, lengthen, and grow once more to meet myself right back where I started, the same, but completely different. All new cells. All of them having forgotten. None of them remembering what I know now.

Prompt: 3 Prompts - Reluctant Protagonist

OH TEACH ME HOW TO CURSE

When you spend as much time around actors as I do
You almost start to believe in the power of words to move the
universe.
Or I do.
Let me speak from my own experience and keep my words out of
your mouth.
I almost started to believe in the power of words to move the
universe.
Not in the way that I think they meant it, but
In some small and significant way, I've always understood the
power of language
There are things that have been said to me that I will never in my
life forget,
Words that have nestled so far into my heart, my blood, my bones
That they are a part of my DNA.
They say that every seven years or so, every single cell in your body
regenerates
Completely
And is new again.
And some people find this important and healing,
Or -
I have found this important and healing.
I do. I have.
I wonder if in seven years those deeply embedded words will begin
also to leave my skin
In a sort of filmy ooze, coming out of my pores like sweat
Like the summer of 2019 when I had just returned from London
And hopped in a car and drove all over, visiting the people and
places I had missed.
I sat outside my AirBnb in Salem MA, drenched in my own sweat
And I watched it run sideways off my arm, like rainwater
And I kept a photo for evidence.

All of that water was inside of me, coming to the surface.
So back to words:
I wonder if one day the poisonous words you spat at me, calmly
As if you were spitting sunflower seed shells into the dirt
Will unstick themselves from my soul
And leave my body, like rainwater.
Like vapor.
Or if every time I see your face, in ten years, in twenty years, in
forty years,
tomorrow:
I will think, "You have cursed me. And it lingers still."
I don't know the remedy for these types of curses, not the way I can
sort of guess at remedies for other things:
Loneliness - a full moon or a warm seashore
Heartache - a fizzy bathtub and a well-written fanfiction
Hunger - food, more acutely eaten after midnight and often pretzels
or cheese
Desire - all kept in a bag i keep zipped and locked beneath my bed
Fear - a heavy frying pan and a well-timed swat
I think in order to defeat a curse or a demon, you must first call it
out by name.
Excuse me: I'll remind myself again.
I think in order to defeat my curses or demons, I must first call
them out by name.
This is difficult, for some days I can barely remember my own.
And some nights, I stare into the darkness of my room and let the
resentment seep into the shadows
And think up at the night sky, "Oh teach me how to curse"
And spit venomed words into the still quiet of my lonely room
Or my frost-cold car.
Like, "You have created the thing that will destroy you"
And "There will come a day when you look at me and see that I
have erased all of the the shit that you smeared into me, and
replaced it with brilliance"

And "Maybe when you look in the mirror, you will recognizes
traces of me in your DNA but I will be long, long gone."
And maybe you will find
Your curses redoubled upon your own soul.
After all
They say that words have power.
And I
I suppose
I do believe it.

Prompt: 3 Prompts - Modern Day Curses

DINNERTIME (DETESTABLE MAW, GAPING MAW, YOUR MAW LIKE MINE)

Yumyumyumyumyum.
I can eat everything that I want to eat.
Because I am hungry and it is time for me to eat.
Yumyum.
Once I have the taste for a thing, I must have it.
Sometimes it is crackers, sometimes it is a lot of crackers.
Dry things and spicy things and things that hurt when you swallow them down.
Have you heard of sparkling water?
Like that, I can swallow down liquid nitrogen and dry ice and isopropyl alcohol
At minus 130 degrees Farenheit.
Anything I want to drink, I can drink it.
I can out drink you and then drink your whole blood and bones,
bone marrow racing through my guts like a bone straw treat.
Yumyumyum.
And sometimes if I want, I can digest all of these things
And sometimes if I want, I can let them sit in lumps.
My body becomes a mountain, becomes an earth, becomes the universe.
And the universe, as we all know
is expanding.
Yumyumyumyumyum.
Time to eat.

Prompt: Bring in Music - Heaven is Here (Florence + The Machine)

Dragon's Belly

I sit carving another tooth. This one came down the gullet 3 meals ago, along with a rabbit, an entire wheat field, and half of a moose. None of them in tact, but I am able to pick at the moose meat which retained a nice char from her fiery breath. The tooth I'm carving looks to be a lower molar. I shave it over and over with my hunting knife, now dull from belly acid. Life in the dragon's gut. Who'd have thought it would come to this? It's only my 2nd tooth. The first was a surprise. I thought maybe she had lost a fight. But wouldn't you know, dragons shed their teeth. I assume they regrow. It's an adaptation to all that throat fire. Wears down the enamel. Instead of spitting them out, it seems they swallow them! Well she does anyway, my lady, the dragon beast who swallowed me whole the first day of shotgun season. What are the boys saying now? I keep wondering if she'll get one of them too. It's a hope and a dread. Don't think the miracle of wholeness could happen twice. If Marcus or Jeff cross her path, I don't think they'll wind up down here shaving teeth with me!

Prompt: Write setting as character

Closing the Book

"It's all in a day's work, ma'am," you say with a forced smile. The woman shakes your hand heartily, reiterating her thanks for the hundredth time as she mops at her grateful tears. You extricate yourself from the situation as fast as possible, making a B-line for the pub. On the way, more than a few villagers wave you down to give their congratulations on your latest heroic adventure. You chat with them all, calling them by their first names, referring to old war stories or complimenting their spouses on the dinner they made you the last time you were over. Finally, you step inside the pub, casting your gaze around the crowded room. Everyone inside turns and raises their goblets to you, sending up a cheer.

You feel the book close.

A relieved rush of air flows through the bar, and everyone puts down their tankards and goes back to their conversations, released from the influence of the Story. You finally let the forced smile drop, your shoulders falling along with it. You've barely got enough energy to stand, but somehow you limp your way to your usual seat at the bar.

"Hey Francis. The usual?" Anthony, the barkeep and owner of this establishment, doesn't even wait for your answer before loading up a plate with mashed potatoes and some kind of meat, sliding your pint of ale down the counter when he's done. You nod your thanks and tuck in.

Eating and drinking are hardly ever interesting, so they rarely make it into the Story. Once or twice you'll have an encounter at the pub, or meet with a client over a drink. But then the Story isn't really about the eating, it's about what's happening around the eating. Heading to the pub after an Adventure is one of the few ways you know to get a break from the Story.

You chug about half the ale in one go, then set it down with a sigh that goes all the way to the soles of your shoes.

"I don't know how much longer I can keep this up, Anth."

Anthony glances over to you, bemused. "As long as people keep reading the Story, I expect."

"I don't remember the last time I had two days to myself," you say with your mouth half full of potatoes, steadfastly ignoring Anthony. "I keep doing the same thing, over and over. Liberate the town. Rescue the Princess. Go treasure hunting in the Caves. Hunt the Dragon..." You gesticulate wildly with your fork to emphasize your points. "Aren't they bored of it by now? Every Princess is the same, every town has the same gang of ruffians, every cave the same kind of treasure. Why keep rehashing the Story when nothing ever really changes?"

"Does the rest of the Party feel the same? Georgio? Ashona? Torg?" Anthony isn't really looking at you, as he already knows the answer. You've come here complaining to him more nights than you care to remember. But he still asks, polishing his bar and speaking to you softly, and he still listens, Gods be thanked.

You heave a great sigh. "Not....exactly. They get bored sometimes, but the grind doesn't bother them the way it bothers me. For the most part..."

"They think it's fun," Anth finishes for you. "All the accolades, the never ending loot, the thankful princesses. They like being in the Story."

You stare moodily into your tankard for a moment before downing the rest of its contents. "Traitors." Anthony chuckles, extricating your mug from your hands and bringing you a new one. "I just want to...I don't know, to relax! To rest on my laurels, for a while. Spend my afternoons doing something mundane for once. Like gardening, or, or..."

"Knitting?" Anth offers unhelpfully. You throw your hands up.

"Sure! Knitting! With some regular ass yarn, not The Golden Thread of The Sacred Whatever. Read a book by the fire - a mystery or a romance or something, not The Ancient Tome of the Lost City Of Whocares."

"You, sitting by the fire reading a romance novel?" Anths' voice is sarcastic, but kind.

"I'm just tired." You collapse onto the bar, pushing your now clean plate aside. "We've made so much money. We've saved so many people. We've stopped or won so many wars. Can you really blame me for dreaming of a quiet retirement?"

Anthony is quiet for a moment, letting you stew in your frustration. He tosses his polishing cloth over his shoulder and drags over his stool, so he can sit at eye level with you on the other side of the bar. "Why do they keep reading the Story, do you think?" he asks quietly. "What could they possibly get out of reliving the same Adventures over and over?"

You groan into your arms. "Their life is boring? They're lazy and unimaginative? They've got nothing better to do? They can't go on Adventures themselves, so they watch us do it to make themselves feel better."

Anthony nods thoughtfully, stealing a swig from your mug. You start to protest, then shake your head with a little grin.

"Maybe you're right," he says, wiping the corner of his mouth with the back of his hand. "Maybe they're unable to go on Adventures, for some reason. They're not strong enough, or brave enough…or they're too old, or young, or sick, or injured." You wave a hand at him dismissively, but he ignores you, continuing. "They've got time to kill because their own lives are unremarkable, or they're stuck in a life that's dissatisfying but they don't feel they can do anything to change it. They revisit the Story over and over with only little adjustments, trying to get everything just right. Reliving happy memories and making new choices to see what, if anything, changes."

You prop your chin on your hands, squinting up at him. "They can't go on Adventures themselves, so they try to live vicariously through us. It's pathetic!"

"Don't you think it could be…I don't know, comforting? Reassuring? To look at an event and know who are the good guys, who are the bad guys, what's going to happen and who is going to win. The Princess will be saved. The King will end the war. The plucky heroes will be rewarded."

"You think I'm plucky?" You grin wolfishly.

Anth just keeps looking at you in that calm way of his, and you roll your eyes, relenting. "So what? So…they like that it's the same every time? They want nothing to change?"

"Maybe. Maybe it feels good to live a life that isn't theirs for a time. Maybe the only chance they have at adventure is when they're watching you. Maybe by living the Story, you're allowing them to…relax by the fire, so to speak."

"So I'm…what, providing a service? Doing a good deed by just letting the Story play out one more time?"

Anth shrugs, rising and pushing back his stool, collecting your empty plate and carrying it to the wash basin at the other end of the bar. You follow him, trailing one hand along the polished wood and thinking. Anthony finally turns back to you and sighs.

"I know it's hard for you, I'm not trying to tell you it's not. But you said it yourself - there's gotta be a reason they keep returning to the Story even though we all know how each Adventure will end. And if they keep returning, then…I guess it's important to them."

You run a hand through your hair absently, rolling Anth's idea over in your mind. You've never tried to imagine what it might be like on the other side of the Story. Why would you? The Story is your life and your life is the Story, what benefit is there to imagining anything else? But if all you want to do is curl up by the fire with a book, which will allow you to relax and escape your current situation…

You take the deepest breath you've taken in weeks, and slam your fist down on the bar. "Okay!" Anthony startles and glares at you reproachfully. "I…guess you have a point. It wouldn't make sense for them to keep coming back if it wasn't important to them. And I guess I can understand why they might enjoy the same Adventures more than once." You rub the back of your neck.

"And I guess it's pretty cool of me to provide them with this diversion, and I am pretty good at it." Anthony raises an eyebrow at you. "I'm also handsome, and brave." He rolls his eyes, but he's grinning.

Then, you feel a pull in your gut. From the way everyone else in the bar shifts, they feel it too. That sensation is as familiar to every one of you as breathing: the book is being opened.

The wave of exhaustion and dread that you're expecting doesn't come. Instead you feel...resolute. Reaffirmed, refreshed, recontextualized. For the first time in many, many Adventures, you feel ready for the Story.

Anth reaches over and squeezes your arm. You smile at him, a thank you in your eyes if not on your lips. He grins, shrugs, and moves back to his customary place in the middle of the bar. You check your clothes, adjust your sword in its scabbard, and smile wide as you feel the Story begin to unfold around you.

Prompt: 3 Prompts - Reluctant Protagonist

The Couch

 I had an idea.

I envision a couch. It is better than my couch at home. My couch used to be blue denim like out past the sandbar of the Atlantic ocean on a cloudy day; now it's more like old jeans. And it was never firm to begin with, but these days it's all compacted fluff. My couch came with an additional cardboard box, the height of a person, filled with fluff. Every year during spring cleaning I take handfuls of fluff from this person-height box and feed the zippered mouths of the cushions. Then I spend another year squashing them down with the length of my body. The cycle goes on. That's my couch.

The couch in my idea is tall. It has two bottom cushions made of firm, hypoallergenic foam. The fabric cover is maroon, thick, soft, high thread count, nothing plastic, with a delicate pattern in subtle colors like an old Persian rug. The back of the couch is also doubly thick and extra firm – plush, and sturdy. This couch sits in the middle of a room at the back of a temple. There are bronze wash-basins beside soft linen blankets and blown glass vases filled with dry and fragrant tree limbs. At the edges of the room sit platters of salt and of clay. Two guards rest at the door of the room and five attendants move about the room. There is a long line of people weaving through the back hallways of the temple.

This is the room of the sick. In this room, a person who has been sick for a very long time, and may continue to be sick for a very long time, lays on the couch. They are wrapped in light, gentle fabric. Their hair was washed and their skin oiled by the attendants. They lays on their side, looking out to the line of people, head supported on a freshly-filled pillow.

A few at a time, the people approach the sick. Sometimes they talk, sometimes they sit in silence. Sometimes, the people ask for her advice; how do I deal with this hardship? How do we settle this wrong? Sometimes they ask about him. What is happening right now in his body? Others just sit with them.

Some people come because they are lost and far from home. Their friend went here once, or their boss recommended it. For whatever reason, today is the day to visit the sick. It's so slow in here, nobody is really in a rush. The temperature is good and the air smells clean, because it's heavily filtered. Sometimes people are afraid to approach the sick, but they are welcome to sit in the room for a while anyway. It's a big room.

Some people come because they are sick too. Maybe in the body, maybe in the mind or the heart. It's nice to see someone like them placed high on a couch and listened too.

The person on the couch is exalted and also, exhausted. They are attended to like a holy being. They are given so much because they have so much to give on this day. It takes everything they have to be here, present with the visitors on the floor, responding to personal questions, receiving many kinds of attention, offering not advice, but a kind of space for whatever people bring with them. Sometimes the person on the couch is unable to speak, and simply lies with eyes closed, breathing and nodding, listening. Demonstrating how to be with pain that doesn't leave.

There are rules about how to approach the person laying on the couch. One doesn't touch or reach out. One doesn't take too much time, doesn't ask for what that person can't give. Just like when you talk to God, you never know what you're going to get.

But the sick people who sign up to spend a half day on the couch aren't gods. They are just people who know a lot about doing hard things every day for many days at a time without a certain end in sight. They are accustomed to being pitied and questioned, and disbelieved. They spend most of their time in hiding, on their own beds and couches, and then on hospital beds, and those sterile pleather waiting room chairs. This is a hard day of work for them. But it is also a gift.

People who cannot reach their own gods today come to the room with the couch. They spend some time breathing in the good air, remembering what they have and where they have been and where they could be. They visit the person on the couch who is both mysterious and elevated, and so painfully real with their eyelashes and breath just 5.5 feet away.

And after some time,

After the worlds of the sick and the worlds of the well-enough intersect around this very tall and supportive couch,

they depart.

Prompt: Touching Luxury

SOMETHING ABOUT

being nineteen - the year that i got really into one direction
that summer - home from college, at my friend keira's house
one thing came on the radio, by the pool
my friend bess, short for elizabeth, says "i love one direction
i can tell them apart by their voices
liam is singing
now it's harry
zayn
and louis and niall sing the second chorus
niall is irish"
i look them up on wikipedia, then youtube
at first i just want to be able to tell them apart too
why are liam and louis so hard to remember which is which
and that's how it starts

i will build an altar on the bones of the fangirls who came before
me
i will take communion in the form of pulsating crowds and sweat
and too loud speakers
i am going to eat the energy of wembley stadium, put all right down
into my belly, where i can keep it safe
maybe this is the way godzilla was formed, on boy bands and light
sticks and fireworks over london
just you wait you wait and see

two nights ago i slipped through the doors of the dubois-robeson
communist bookstore
it's a $10 suggested donation and i give it because i have ten dollars
in my wallet
the backroom is small and cool and a black and white poster of
lenin glowers wisely over the mighty gathering
this music sucks ass

i hate it - dissonant, messy, PLAY A CHORD (I WANT TO
SHAKE THIS PERSON BY THEIR SHOULDERS) PLAY A
GODDAMN CHORD
the bands are small and disorganized and the feedback is a priest at
confession
MAKE IT STOP please someone with TECH KNOWLEDGE
make it STOP

the music starts, and this song is about being gay
this song is about war
this song is about the occupation of palestine
this song is about the ugliness of humanity
this song is about capitalism
this is a love song it was based on true events
this song is happening but no one can hear it because the mic
volumes are all wrong and there's FEEDBACK someone figure
out the GODDAMN feedback
my fingers in my ears i pray to the poster of lenin for silence and
balance in sound
but there is no mercy in this place, there are no london telephone
booths
and one direction dissolved in 2015
but as for this music this place the things we are making
just you wait you wait and see

Prompt: Spiritual experience at a concert

You Do It For Her

Forgiveness looks like knees open, ankles crossed lazily. A moment of sustained eye contact without both your butts clenching. Someone gets up to get a glass of water, comes back and sits down. Comfortable silence. Cold winter light slipping through a window. A palm down on the arm of the sofa.

Someone comes to the door, no thank you. The comfortable silence resumes. Someone picks up a book. Another thing comes up and they turn it over, this time with more gentleness and fewer words than before.

Someone goes abroad and gets engaged. A wedding is planned but the plans crack. Sitting on the floor again in a new country this time. The floor is tile. The butter and eggs live on the counter. The milk comes in a box. This time forgiveness sits in the other room while the broken bride weeps into her wine glass. Eventually forgiveness comes in and it's all giggles. Wet, salty, sobby giggles over rosemary crackers from a tube with a foreign name.

Forgiveness travels back home where it is stretched thin, across state lines. Thin as a telephone wire, thin as the word, K. Thin as the hole in the jeans she let you borrow and you forgot to give back and she didn't care because she was happy at the time for you to have them.

The only way to break forgiveness is to forget or pretend it never happened. Forgiveness does break sometimes, because they do forget, each of them, getting lost in their own worlds. But something snaps them back and it's usually the smell of children's Tylenol or getting to the last post-it note of the pack. And they don't call right away but they are back on the trail of forgiveness again. Forgiveness looks like trying. When you can't do it for yourself, you do it for her. You don't tell her and she never sees it. But the next time she calls and you're wearing a clean work outfit with a nude lipstick and you got paid, and she's part of that, forgiveness looks like that too.

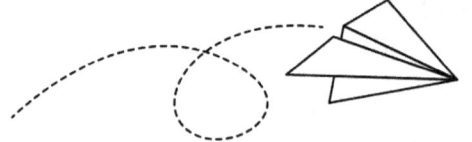

Prompt: What does forgiveness look like?

What Does Forgiveness Look Like?

Tangled, tangled.

Confused, and tired, and over it.

Sobbing in the middle of the night, curled up under the covers,

hugging your favorite teddy bear from when you were six.

     A ball of twine so knotted and tied up inside you;

     that you've spend years trying to suss apart;

     that your friends have tried to help you untangle;

     that your therapist has teased a foot or two of

  string out of;

     that your spouse lovingly tries to run their

     fingers through even though they often

  snag.

Feeling like every bit of string is of equal importance and must be

preserved, — — — — — — — — — — — — — —

untangled & pressed & neatly sewn back into your understanding

of self. — — — — — — — — — — — — — — —

That feeling suddenly giving way to the knowledge that if you just

  cut

    the ball

      in half,

        the pieces will untangle themselves.

A gasp, and a sigh.

The wave of relief and sorrow as the blade slices through, so sharp,

so sharp. — — — — — — — — — — — — — —

Little scraps of string falling away, your desire to hold tight

to them gone. — — — — — — — — — — — — —

Like picking up the scraps that are meaningful and tieing them

back together into a shape that looks more like you.

For a time it looks like walking through your life shedding little bits of string, finding pieces stuck on your sweater with static electricity and carefully pulling them off to throw in the garbage. Like your friend pulling one off your back from where you couldn't see it. Like your spouse brushing one from your hair and asking you if it's important. Like your therapist remarking how much lighter you seem without that dense ball of twine weighing you down.

Forgetting. Or not forgetting, but not needing to remember. Of remembering time spent untangling and not hating yourself for spending it.

Shock. Confusion at the way your body moves now. Feeling like you're breathing air for the first time in years. Laughing.

Of moving through several weeks or months or years forgetting you even had a tangled mess of a ball of string, before being overwhelmed with a sense of loss for no longer having it. Moving through that loss and accepting that it's not wrong to mourn for something just because it was harmful to you.

The calm stillness of a morning when you wake up, run your fingers along the thread of yourself, feeling those bumps where you've tied yourself back together, and feeling that this is right, this is what you are supposed to feel like, like this is how you want to feel.

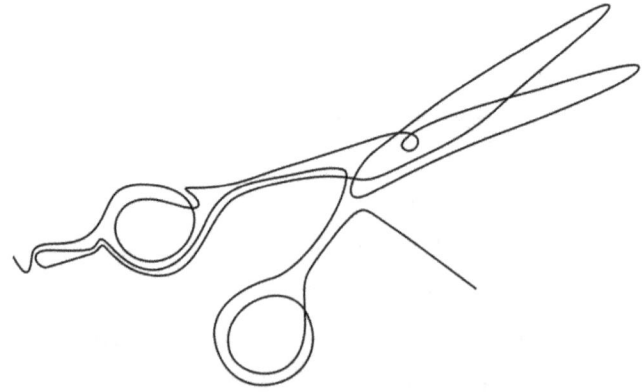

Prompt: What does forgiveness look like?

TRI

A triptych is a work of art (usually a panel painting)
that is divided into three sections.
"I've seen this one," I say.
"In person?" He asks.
"In person, yeah."
The title is The Garden of Earthly Delights, by Hieronymus Bosch
and it was painted in 1490(ish)
"Can you believe his name is Hieronymus Bosch? Hieronymus
Bosch.
It sounds like something out of an Eva Ibbotson novel.
Dianna Wynn Jones. Well, maybe not her. Someone like-"
"Where did you see it?" He asks.
"I don't remember," I say.
"It can't have been London. Maybe Italy? I only saw those
cartoons in -"
"Madrid?" He asks.
"Madrid. Can't have been. I've never been to Spain."
"Then you haven't seen it," He says. "It's been there since 1939."
"Oh."
He closes the Wikipedia tab.

"Hieronymus Bosch is a good name though. Want to go to a
museum?"
"What, now?" It's raining, although it's always on the edge of rain
in London.
It's the only thing that feels like culture shock to me, in England.
Developing an understanding of the London rain.
I was told for years that it's always raining, and I didn't realize
people mean it's never raining.
Not really.

There's mist and constant drizzle and always puddles and holes in

my sneakers that lead to wet socks.
But never rain.

Once, there was a lightning storm and we sat on my bed half naked
to watch it,
Electricity forking across the sky.
The glass doors out to the small patio created a triptych I liked
Window blinds, glass door with skyline, glass door with skyline.
I don't want to leave my house today.
He doesn't live here, he's only visiting and can do whatever he likes.
"Yes, now."
I've almost forgotten what we're talking about.

"Don't you want to do things? I feel like we're always just sitting
around when we're not at school."
It didn't used to be like that before I started dating you, I don't say.
I used to go places all the time. Like the zoo and the opera and the
late night museum openings where I did my fingerprints at a
forensics table and left so much oily residue that the man running it
told me never to commit a crime, walks to Camden along the locks,
never actually took a boat (or did I?), social dances where I spoke
to more people in three hours than I would a full week of school
and
"I'm tired," I say.
It's both true and not true and some other third thing.

"Try being twenty-five sometime."
Sometimes he thinks this is funny and sometimes he does not and
sometimes he looks at me with some other thing in his eyes that
forecasts the day he will leave me.
"I think I'm going to head out," He says.
The few times I visit his house, I am shocked by the walk.
Even if he never loved me or if he only thought he did or if he did,
it's a hike.

I think of him walking and me lying on my bed and school the
point around which our obtuse points triangulate and think of how
words have multiple meanings or one or none or-
  1. of an angle more than 90 degrees and less than 180
  2. annoyingly insensitive or slow to understand.
  3. not sharp-pointed or sharp-edged; blunt.
I am all of these things, sprawled across my bed
on my cabbage flower patterned sofa in my London flat
that I share with two roommates I hardly see but resent
Perhaps the feeling is mutual, I think, as lightning forks across the
skyline in my memory
We three moved into a two-bedroom flat with a living room, after
all.

Guess in which room I live.

Prompt: Third spaces

Das Ist Eine Buch

The bookstore was small and quiet. There's just about enough room to walk between the tall shelves, piled high with books and memorabilia. The floor above you was a theater, and outside on the cobble streets, across a wide flat road, was one of the most famous opera houses in Austria. The next door over from the shop was the Theater Gift Shop, with posters and playbills and bookmarks and things. On the gift shop's far side was the ticket office.

The shop isn't associated with the theater, but it made sense for there to be a bookshop here. It had a nice theater section – opera scripts and framed production photos. And plenty of kitsch, like Shakespeare bobble heads and themed stationary. But it also had this nice little kids book section. Coloring books and photo books, German translations of Harold's Purple Crayon and Goodnight Moon. It felt nice to thumb through them, familiar colorful pictures with unfamiliar text beside them.

You were supposed to be attending an opera performance, but you did a little too much strolling around the city and tickets were sold out by the time you got there. It was disappointing, and you'd ducked into the shop to see if they had anything that would cheer you up or inspire you to start on another adventure. Your honeymoon has very little structure, just an idea of what you might like to do each day, which sometimes meant missing the opera but also meant that you could follow whatever inspiration struck your fancy.

Your partner's been at the other end of the bookstore looking for a specific opera score, and as he moved back toward you it seems he hadn't found it. You'd both felt a little lighter coming in here, the familiar scents and sounds of a bookstore crossing the language barrier and putting you at ease, erasing some of the frustration at having missed your show. But nothing in here had quite grabbed your attention either, and your lifted moods were beginning to flag once more. Your partner was moving toward you with an air of defeat, resignation that this afternoon was a bust.

He moved close enough that you could speak in hushed voices. Not that you have to, it just always seems the polite way to converse in a bookstore. Your shoulders brushed as he entered your personal bubble, a comfortable warm presence, and he nodded to the book in your hands, asking what it was. You'd just picked up the next book on the children's shelf without really noticing. Das Ist Eine Buch. A First Words book, a board book, with beautiful art and a playful, silly style. It made both of you smile, his German good enough to read you the few scant words per page.

The whole mood changed. The book made you laugh.

Should we get it, he asked?

It's a children's book, you said. It's for kids.

Yeah well…. he started. We could save it. You know, for later.

Your eyes lit up as they met his, shining. Your mind suddenly filled with the clearest image: a small peach painted bookshelf lined with books, toys, and stuffed animals. Low enough to the ground for little hands to reach out and grab. Books from each of your childhoods next to the new ones you'd buy together. Well loved copies of classics next to indestructible board books. This book in your hands being the first you placed on the shelf.

Really? You ask. We don't have anything…else.

But we could start, he says.

There's an energy between you now, an electricity, a joy. The malaise of your afternoon is gone, replaced by the thrill of looking to the future. You hold the book close to your chest.

Alright, you say. Yeah, let's do it.

He grins broadly and grabs your hand, and you move to the checkout.

Prompt: Bring in an object

FALSE EYELASHES AND FISHNETS: OR HAVE YOU EVER FELT THE INEXPLICABLE AND EXQUISITE SADNESS OF LEANING AGAINST THE RUBBER WALL OF THE HIGH SCHOOL GYMNASIUM AND WISHING SOMEONE WOULD CALL OUT YOUR NAME, PERHAPS TO DANCE AT THE SENIOR PROM UNDER THE TACKY DISCO LIGHTS OR PERHAPS SIMPLY TO PLAY IN A FOURTH-PERIOD KICKBALL GAME, ANY POSITION WILL DO, ONLY PLEASE DON'T CALL ME LAST?

No one ever expects the Fish, in their snakeskin coat
Gliding silently up to the curb on their motorbike
Helmet buckled securely under their chin
Wind-swept curls sticking in False Eyelashes
And eyes that Goggle, Huge and Luminous in the moonlight.
I certainly didn't.

It was a Thursday, a school night, and I had calculus homework to finish.
"Finish" is a nebulous word, that mainly meant somehow type out as much of the math equation into a Google search as I could, and then hit enter and hope against hope that someone on Yahoo Answers! had the same problem back in 2010, or whenever.

I'm stuck on a problem, because I can't figure out how in God's

name to put an exponent into a search engine. I'm halfway through searching "how to put an exponent into a search engine" when the first rock hits my window. Tap.
It's loud enough that I know it's not nothing, but quiet enough that I know it's not the woodpecker who has decided that my windowsill is the ideal place to build their nest.I'm trying to decide if I care enough to get up and look, when the second rock hits my window. Tap.

I'm across the floor in a bundle of blankets, before I have to worry about overcoming my laziness. My textbook gets caught in the pull of my blanket
cape and thuds to floor, loudly. It doesn't matter. Mom works the night-shift at the hospital, and I'm the only one home.

The moon is huge and full, and in the pale light that glints off my windowpane I see small glimpses of glimmers, spots of sparkle.
It all shifts into gear in an instant. These aren't rocks. They're scales.

When I was very young, I remember a hot summer day, where you stand on the basketball court and aren't sure if your shoes are shoes or just a gloopy extension of the concrete. The kind of day when you yank yourself home and wash off the sticking tar in soap water dishes before coming near the threshold of your house. I'm wearing a white t-shirt and two identical yellowed armpit rings of sweat, and I can feel the skin on the bridge of my nose burning red, and I can already hear the scolding I'm going to get from Mom for forgetting my cap. Again.

Nic is the captain of the green team, and Kloss is the captain of the Levitating Wizards, which I'm not sure yet if it's a dumb name or not. Wizards might be good at some parts of basketball, like magically getting the ball into the hoop and confusing the other team with magic or whatever, but the levitating is a bit tricky. Would levitating through the air with the ball count as traveling? I'm working on deciding if it does or not, when I realize it's quiet on the court.

Everyone is looking at me.

"What are you dreaming about?"

"Nothing - who's team am I on?"

"We got an odd number. You can be the ref if you want."

No one wants to be the ref. It's a death sentence. Kel was the last ref and they were so honest about it that the game ended with 6 fist fights, a screaming match, and an undisputed winner, and no one would talk to Kel. They ended up transferring at the end of the year.

I'm not so dumb.

"I'll be bench."

No one cares. They already started playing a few minutes ago.

It's no good to be bench near the court. People'll only use it as an excuse to clobber you with the ball and say "It's not out because it bounced off your stupid face ahaha"

So I sit down by the Crickle.

The Crickle is a tiny flood of water that too small to even be called a crick, but not so small as a puddle. It's muddy, and one time some older kids tried to build a dam there with a bunch of chewed up gum and ended up flooding the

whole park. I don't know where all that water came from, but no one messes with the Crickle anymore. Some kids say that if you wish on the Crickle, it'll come true. And some say that if you wish on the Crickle you'll be visited by a ghostly half-man-half-fish with no hands and huge holes where his eyes, ears, and mouth should be and he'll suck your soul for his dinner.

I don't know yet what I believe.

Prompt: False eyelashes and fishnets

Lush

The island where I live is said to be a place where many lay lines cross. Lives intersect in a way that seems spontaneous at first, but after some time has passed, the parties will swear it was fate. You meet a man crossing a back porch barefoot humming to himself, and then you squeeze past him in a crowded sixth floor hallway in Chelsea. Young strangers in Egypt meeting their first camels find they are wearing the same dog shirt from the same boat café. A family from Mumbai shares a fenugreek-spiced roti with the bookshop workers on their lunch-break. Their cousins all end up at the same university in Italy later that year.

Others say this place is more like the Bermuda triangle or the land of Hades. Some people end up there accidentally, while others come intentionally to disappear. There is thought to be a force-field around the island that forces some to lose their brains en route, causing them to forget that standing in the middle of a highway can be dangerous, and walking into a restaurant naked is inappropriate, and stealing ice cream from a locked shop results in prison time (even if it's only for a couple of hours).

Everyone has a different theory about this place. Some think it's an absolute delight and others find it to be a trap. My theory is somewhere in the middle. This place is lush. It is a cultural swamp. And by swamp I do not mean uninhabitable. I mean a place so fecund, so damp with life-giving waters, so starved for ideas and connections that the ecosystem is packed full, constantly erupting with all kinds of new life. Seeds bloom with intoxicating ease. You have only to say the word aloud to the air and someone has grabbed it and planted it in the ground. You have but to meet three other people in a room and suddenly you have a company. Space can be found, supplies bought, funds donated, people engaged.

The downside to a place like this, and the thing rarely acknowledged, is rot. This place molds. I don't know if it's the perpetual moisture in the air or the lack of initial toil required to grow things, but boy do things start to disintegrate quickly. Pruning is not popular here. Let people grow as they please, wander where they like, work how they want. The old ways. Poisons develop. Like I said, rot.

I used to believe that a person could only spend so much time here before their minds and morals would subtly but irrevocably start to rot. Well, whatever that time limit, I've certainly exceeded it. I am no longer an objective observer. I fear that people can smell it on me when I go off island. She lacks boundaries, her jokes are unsavory, she's drawn to chaos. I try to keep it hidden: the pedophilia, the culty behavior, the barely-hidden signs of abuse that surrounded me as a kid. I'm afraid that it gives off an odor like an unchecked lily. I'll never be cosmopolitan, but I try, try not to rot.

Prompt: Second Intersection

Do You Ever Wish You Had Cancer?

a poem about chronic illness

Do you ever wish you had cancer?

Do you ever wake up in the middle of the night,
Sitting straight up in bed, gripping your body in pain,
Biting back a yelp or a curse trying not to wake your partner,
Sleeping so freely beside you?

Do you ever wish for a devouring virus,
Eating your bones from within, constricting your veins,
Poisoning your blood, a wasting disease leaving holes in your body,
To prove where it had been?

Do you ever wish for chemicals,
Injected into your blood, radiated through your skin,
Dozens of colorful medications dispensed into your palm to
Wash down with your morning coffee?

Do you ever spend days feeling so hungry and eating nothing,
Limping through the hours with no fuel for your body,
Forcing down a snack to survive your workday and paying for it by
Spending the rest of the day swallowing bile?

Do you ever spend hours standing in the bathroom,
Hair pulled back, knuckles white against the porcelain,
Praying to every god you can think of to just make it stop,
Waiting to see if you'll spill your guts across the floor?

Do you ever wish you had something to point to,
To blame for your pain, to explain your weakness, to prove
Consistency constancy, with symptoms and treatments,
that you can utter like a Prayer to explain:

This is what's wrong?

This is what's wrong.

Do you ever wish you had cancer?

Prompt: After 5 months of doctors visits, tests, bloodwork, scans, and thousands of dollars, I was told yet again that everything was negative and nothing was wrong. I was having a really bad pain and nausea and depression day and this fell out of me

Caramel

I spent last night elbow deep in caramel. I've never done caramel before. It looks hard on tv, always crystallizing or burning. I prefer chocolate. Or butter and plain sugar beat until velvetine and spreadable. Even a sweet, crunchy peanut butter blob atop a tablespoon has more appeal than caramel. What is it, if not near-burned sugar and magic. Caramel is for people who own candy-thermometers. Chemists. Pencil pushers. Foodies. And candy queens. Nobody Makes caramel. // But I did. Last night. I found a recipe and I followed. Simmering clear plastic goo like liquid bubble wrap, I thought, how on earth could this congeal into something golden and painterly? But from underneath the slimy clear bubbles a color grew. It was the color of Nutella, at the bottom of my pan. Shit, I thought, it's burnt. But then it began to spread and lighten. And in four and a half seconds it came off the heat, golden bubbles smacking their mouths open wide to receive a splash of cream. I dumped all the cream in at once, which you are not supposed to do. Slowly pour in the cream, whisking vigorously. Well that, my friends, is a three handed task. You need one hand to pour, one hand to whisk, and one hand to hold the spinning pot steady. So in went the heavy cream in one heavy splash, followed by lava-like bursts and sizzles of hot sugar. Whisk whisk whisk. Fuck fuck fuck, it's hard, it's congealing, it's sticking to my whisk! And then, like magic, it released. Warm golden pool of almost caramel gliding counter clockwise like a lazy whirlpool. Pats of butter plopped in. Back on the hot burner to whisk even more. Then suddenly, it's done. Left to cool. And taste. Toasty. Snappingly sweet. Caramel.

Prompt: 3 Prompts - What is your catnip?

REVE'NGE

This is some Count of Monte Crisco level bullshit.

An apple pie you can feel all the way to your toes.

I'm going to regret this later, on the toilet at 3 AM but right now I'm in heaven.

The neon letter E gives one last precious gasp and flickers out.

OK. Make that Heav'n.

Touch everyone, but make eye contact with no one. Or vice versa.

I put on new socks today and my shoes squeak with every gummy step forward.

A murder chorus of mice beneath patent leather heels.

Squeak squeak squeak.

Would I like to dance? No, I wouldn't.

What's my name? I'd tell you, but I'd have to kill you.

That's a joke. Or is it. I don't know. Did you laugh?

Prompt: 3 Prompts - What is your catnip?

We Are So Full Of Light

Everyone has that one thing that makes them go apeshit. You could be having a completely normal day at work, you're interacting with coworkers, and bam - that one song comes on the radio. You're at a party, chatting up your roommate's best friend's sister's fiance, and boom - you smell the cookies in the oven. You're unwrapping presents at Christmas with your whole family and pow - you get some fuzzy socks with that super soft fluff. And now you're quickly excusing yourself from the water cooler and dancing your way back to your desk. You're clearing your little paper plate of cheese and crackers and checking the kitchen timer. You're throwing the wrapping paper aside and luxuriating in the pillowy softness. These things just get deep inside you. They're usually associated with one of the senses - hearing, smell, touch. And being exposed to them just absolutely transports you into another space. It's physically impossible to keep your body still while listening to That One Song. It's absolutely absurd not to eat three chocolate chip cookies warm out of the oven. It's preposterous to believe you aren't going to rub those socks on your face. Sometimes it's because they remind you of something - the time you saw that band live, baking with your grandparents, being snuggled up in bed with the person you love most. But sometimes it's none of those. It's just about the raw essence of the thing, that catnip quality being married to the thing itself, not in reference to another pleasurable experience but conjuring and embodying the experience by existing in the first place. And I love that.

Prompt: 3 Prompts - What is your catnip?

A Vineyard Sail

Feet browned like an expensive wood stain, with callouses softened by sand, I watched him alight on the rim of the vessel like a spring bug on a leaf. There are two of them, old friends. One brought me roses last week. The other I've been sleeping with since July. It's now late August and the boys are taking me sailing. It's not what you think.

Sliding through the harbor takes ages. We nearly glide into several yachts, their owner's necks red with top shelf drink. The sun pools on our white sails and tells the breeze where to touch. I watch them both. One with his reflexes, so swift he's approaching flight. The other, the one who's bed I shared, simply lifts it up and puts it down. It being whatever obstacle is in his way. I like watching this brute display of force. It makes me laugh because there is a softness, a gentleness so deeply hidden, that creeps out in the night and asks me how I am and do I like it. On the boat, with another man here, that softness exists only in my memory of him, and perhaps, when I let myself think about it, what might happen later tonight.

I'm in pink, a color I like because it is also the color of my summer skin. I don't like making choices about what to wear - I lose myself entirely in trying to send the right codes. But when I'm already this close to naked, the textured two piece pinching my hips might as well be pink. The swift one asks if I want to hold the rudder now that we are out of the harbor, away from other people. He looks at me through his salty curls. He becomes the teacher, an air of equanimity suddenly in his voice, as if there were thirty other pupils instead of just me. This too is a form of preening. He's aware that his experience, his mastery, is well-known in the harbor. He has a gift, everyone says. He somehow shares a language with the boats. There is something in the way he dances up and down the length of this tiny sailboat, like Peter Pan taunting his shadow, and he'll never fall.

While the one flits under the bough, behind my back, below deck and back again with sparkling drinks, the other just sits. He looks far, and gives nothing away. I may not even exist. I've crossed his eye line intentionally three times

now and only once did he blink in my direction - as if I were an unwanted fish. But this is part of it too. It's a game and the game is, who is the better actor. Who can give nothing away.

I'm terrible at this game. I'm giving it all away, to both of them. I lift my eyelashes until they touch the bones of my face, giving both men a look of such exhilaration and awe. I am nothing if not a generous guest.

Prompt: Romance on a boat

Brandy, You're a Fine Girl

How many times have I watched them sail away. What an incredible cliché that I get to live. Really what better way to button up a relationship or a fling than to watch him swallowed up by a gargantuan steel vessel, gliding out of the harbor, off to his next chapter by way of the mainland, the big country, the world. And I turn the page to my next chapter.

It was a cliché I relished as a child when I first heard Brandy, You're a Fine Girl by Looking Glass at age 9 and instantly thought they were talking about the popstar Brandy in Cinderella. I pictured her in white blouse with a blue sapphire necklace, sloshing pints delicately somehow. I hoped— no, I could never... but I hoped one day I could be as beautiful as Brandy who takes care of all the rugged men in the salty port town.

It seemed so romantic in that song: booze and brine and blood all flowing through their veins as one. The men could escape; the women couldn't. What else was new. Then in high school I was introduced to the Portuguese tradition of Fado music. Never heard it? Google it. It will reach in through your heart, grasp your soul and give it a good hard squeeze. Fado is a style of music that was developed to express the agony of waiting, longing for your man lost at sea. It was traditionally sung by women in the ages of Portuguese "exploration" and conquest, and is still performed in Fado houses today. It is exquisite. You've never heard anguish so beautiful and timeless.

One thing though Tessa, I remind myself, these guys are assholes. The "man that Brandy loves," loves the sea more than her. I mean who doesn't love and fear the sea more than humans? But he essentially chooses the unknown, the life of adventure and drink and likely early death over care and security and Brandy! The most beautiful, glass-slippered girl with no agency that there ever was. And these Portuguese ladies were sitting at home waiting around for their slaughterers to return home, knock them up, and leave once more. So what still appeals to me about this tradition of waiting at home for the men to come fuck me and then go off on their adventures?

First of all, home. I am starting to see myself as part of a tradition of sick authors, who are bound to their homes or their rooms in body alone. Like an itchy and bloated Helena, I sit on my soft fabrics, longing to run my fingers along the curled locks of my lover. But I have my women to keep me company. All of us left behind. When he comes home, my stomach will dip and drop again. I will lose sleep. My thighs will become stronger and bruised like a layer of watercolor. I might even be late for work one day. Total, delicious upheaval! I've learned to calm it a little, but still, that's what we hope for from a lover. I delight in caring for him. I pour the rounds when his friends and their friends come around. The looks we sneak between us will sustain me while he is gone. And when he eventually does go – I may cry and sweat and soak deep in salty baths until - the water settles again.

Prompt: 3 Songs

Down the green Hill

Up the graying carpet, the shushes of shuffling feet.
The crunch as someone steps on a leaf blown in
from the open archway, a cool wind occasionally
sending them skittering across the floor.

Sitting on the hard wooden bench, song book in your hands,
folded paper program crinkling as it's gripped too tight.
Low bellowing from the organ, underscored by
hushed voices whispering to one another.

The quick metal sound of zippers being pulled,
hats pulled on and keys jingling as they're pulled out of pockets.
The trumpet sounds of cars unlocking, clunks of doors closing,
the local radio DJs voice briefly audible before windows rolled up.

Park in the small lot next to the cars you followed here.
A quick glance in the window to make sure your face is on right.
A murmured hello to someone you've seen but never met before,
tired smiles, coughing to clear the throat.

Soft thuds as you walk the dirt path, grass cut short to either side.
Carefully planted trees designed to provide shade
during a long service or an anniversary visit.
Wilted flowers laid at the feet of mossy stones.

Remembrances in the voices of the of not-crying,
fresh flowers strewn on a smooth wooden box.
A final goodbye as the motor whirs and turns the winch
and the body is lowered into the earth.

Leaving one by one, touching the arm of someone
you recognize as "family" though you don't know their name.

Some leaving quickly, others lingering, comforted or discomfited by these sorts of things.

Eventually you all descend. Someday this will be a green hill, but for today it's topped with fresh brown dirt.

Prompt: Down the green hill

Prompts

Are there more wheels or doors in the world?

Third spaces
Third spaces are places you interact with others socially outside of work and home

Write the News of the Day

Modern day curses

Greenland
"Greenland" is a catch-all term that we use to describe a devising/writing process that we learned from the Debate Society (Hannah Bos, Paul Thureen, and Oliver Butler) during our time at the National Theater Institute. It involves a lot of writing based on things we collectively know nothing about. To learn more, please email us at weirdsysters@gmail.com

3 Prompts: Fanfic Tropes (Only 1 Bed)
On this day we each brought in a prompt, and each wrote on all three prompts. We thought it would be fun to include all three of our writings on each one here

What is a cult?

Touching Luxury

List of 10 things we know/don't know about

The Quiet Year
The Quiet Year is a role playing game using a deck of cards rather than dice. For this prompt, we played the game as a group, and then used the things that happened in the game as inspiration for our writing

Something about animals

Prompts (continued)

Viewing your homestead from a distance

3 Prompts: Write about a reluctant protagonist

Bring in Music

Write the setting as a main character

Spiritual experience at a concert

What does forgiveness look like?

Bring in an object

False eyelashes & fishnets

Second Intersection

Chronic Illness

3 Prompts: What's your catnip

Romance on a boat

3 Songs Prompt

Down the Green Hill

Ivy Stevens grew up in a small town and moved to a slightly bigger one in Upstate New York, on land belonging to the Gayogohó'no people, where she lives with her supportive husband and cute dog. Her training is in stage management for the theater, which she has done consistently for the past decade, most frequently with the local Shakespeare and opera companies. For a day job, she is the inventory manager at an indie bookstore, where she reads less than you'd think but still a lot. Her goal when writing is to conjure in the reader the sense of being in a particular time and place, which they can then occupy together for a while.

Elena Faverio is a trans nonbinary creative and abolitionist living in Lenapehoking, (present day Philadelphia) with their smoochy cat Yertle. Previous writing includes Blaze (a musical about a pyromaniac in love with the girl next door), i don't get out much (a play with music about people who don't leave their houses), and After the Flood (a musical about siblings and processing grief). Elena is working to abolish policing and the carceral system, and making art as far removed from everything they learned in drama school as possible. More at https://www.youtube.com/c/ElenaFaverio.

Tessa Permar grew up on the island of Noepe (also called Martha's Vineyard) and trained to become a choreographer. At 25, Tessa moved back home to treat chronic Lyme Disease. During this time, she started writing, cooking, and dating. She has since worked as a chocolatier, non-profit worker, and a job coach, supporting individuals with barriers to employment. She will one day escape Martha's Vineyard and be able to buy socks whenever she wants. Until then, she continues to choreograph, teach accessible dance classes, and spend quality time with Ivy and Elena. Find her at: howtobesick.substack.com/